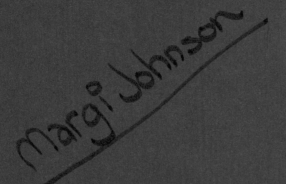

W9-COS-921

# THE CHRISTMAS COLLIE

❧

by Ted Paul

Illustrated by Mary Kummer

*I remember a time*
    *not too long ago,*
*When the air turned cold*
    *and it started to snow.*
*Our fireplace crackled,*
    *our home was alive,*
*Christmas was coming*
    *and I was just five.*

*A Christmas like that,*
　*in all its glory,*
*Begins to record*
　*like a life-long story,*
*To be held in the memory*
　*of those growing old,*
*Until like now,*
　*it begins to unfold.*

*I had been pretty good*
  *all year long,*
*Trying to do right*
  *and not do wrong.*
*I had cleaned my room,*
  *even helped with the dishes,*
*'cause a Christmas puppy*
  *topped all of my wishes.*

*A kite or a train*
    *are really great toys,*
*There are many neat things*
    *that attract small boys,*
*But this year amid tinsel*
    *and green boughs of holly,*
*I hoped and I prayed*
    *I would get my own Collie.*

*On Christmas morning*
*    I dashed to the stair,*
*My Pop sat smiling*
*    in his favorite chair.*
*My eyes took in all,*
*    the whole room at a glance,*
*I was glued to the bannister*
*    as if in a trance.*

*For there on his lap*
    *sat my puppy for sure,*
*A big red bow*
    *between two puffs of fur.*
*With a squeal of excitement,*
    *I came racing down,*
*And off my Dad's lap*
    *the pup came with a bound.*

*At the foot of the stairs*
    *we met with delight,*
*I need hardly say,*
    *it was love at first sight.*
*He jumped in my lap*
    *and licked my face,*
*And I cuddled him close*
    *in a boy-dog embrace.*

*I looked up through paws,*
*   wagging tail and fur,*
*My Mom and my Dad,*
*   they were kind of a blur.*
*Mom with her apron*
*   and Dad with his tie,*
*Were both dabbing something*
*   from under their eye.*

*From that moment on,*
  *we were always together,*

*Summer. . .*

and Winter. . .

*in all kinds of weather.*

*Words can't describe*
*what it means to a boy,*
*To have a real pal*
*instead of a toy.*

We both grew a lot
    in those early years,
Sharing laughter and joy
    and occasional tears.
I remember the measles
    and the long stay in bed,
And my Toby right with me,
    my hand on his head.

He watched me intently,
   his eyes seemed to say,
"Come on – get well,
   it's time to go play!"
When I finally got up
   and he knew I was better,
He was off in a flash
   to fetch me my sweater.

Then he grabbed my jacket
    and raced for the door,
And back for my muffler,
    galoshes and more.
And once outside
    he went flying around,
His antics were those
    of a furry clown.

*He would run right on past me*
*    and skid to a stop,*
*Then crouch like a rabbit*
*    about ready to hop.*
*The minute I moved,*
*    he'd bound off with a smile,*
*We played like that*
*    for what seemed like a mile.*

*Those early school years*
*    really tugged at my heart,*
*Because five days each week*
*    we spent much time apart,*
*At first Toby pouted*
*    and moved extra slow,*
*In his way he was asking,*
*    "Gosh, why can't I go?"*

*But soon weekday mornings,*
*that lovable fool*
*Would bounce on my bed*
*and bark, "Time for school!"*
*After dressing and breakfast*
*and Mother's great fuss,*
*My Toby would then see me*
*down to the bus.*

*I waved goodbye,*
    *riding off with my buddies,*
*Then tried to remember*
    *the coming day's studies.*
*I know that he watched*
    *til we faded from view,*
*Then he trotted on home,*
    *he was part of Dad's crew.*

*He guarded the henhouse,*
*Helped Dad gather sheep.*

*Chased the crows from Mom's garden,*
*Then he'd doze off to sleep.*

But he'd keep one eye open
as he lazed in the sun,
To watch for my schoolbus
and be ready for fun.
And when I returned,
later on in the day,
An overjoyed Collie
was eager to play.

*Hiking or baseball,*
*    we went all the time,*
*And work never phased him,*
*    he was right in his prime.*

*He was a picture-book Collie,*
*a real sight to see,*
*But the years passed too quickly*
*for Toby and me.*

In no time it seemed
    I was off to the war,
And my aging, sad Toby
    saw me off at the door.
I hugged him, blinked hard,
    then looked quickly away,
For I knew at his age
    he could go any day.

*In the hard years that followed,*
*    my Toby passed on,*
*He's in Heaven I know,*
*    herding sheep on God's lawn.*

*And I have a family,*
*a five year old boy,*
*He's happy and healthy,*
*an absolute joy.*

*I have to stop writing,*
    *though it's hard to believe,*
*But I hear my son stirring*
    *and it's late Christmas eve.*
*When he comes down the stairs,*
    *all I want him to see,*

*Is his Toby the Second,*
*his Mommy and me.*

## Acknowledgements

*Our sincere thanks to Larry Reynolds and Barbara McCampbell for the photographs of their beautiful Collies, the models for many of our illustrations. And to Mr. & Mrs. John La Rocca and sons Michael and Matthew, models par excellence, we couldn't have done it without you.*

*To Mary Angela Kummer, our magnificent illustrator, our love and heartfelt thanks. Your God given talent is surpassed only by your love and devotion.*

*Thank you all.*